FIFTY
FASHION
LOOKS
THAT
CHANGED
THE
1970s

**DESIGN
MUSEUM**

FIFTY
FASHION
LOOKS
THAT
CHANGED
THE
1970s

**PAULA
REED**

THE
1970s

Bryan Ferry and Jerry Hall pose together in the Amstel Hotel in 1976 in Amsterdam, the Netherlands. Ferry and Hall were the coolest couple about town and showed that the classical style could still be chic, even amid the stylistic mayhem of the 1970s.

David Bowie and his wife Angie epitomized the decade's near obsession with androgyny, sexuality and sheer, show-stopping glamour. Below: The work of the Scottish designer Bill Gibb encapsulated another major 70s leitmotif – a romantic nostalgia for nature and exotic folk cultures. Here Twiggy models a swirling dress of checkerboard and flowers.

THE 1970s

This was the decade of women's lib. Key figures such as Betty Friedan and Germaine Greer set the sociological agenda. But women were a long way from gaining confidence about their place in the world. In fact, a look back at the fashion of the decade gives a startlingly clear view of the deep-seated uncertainties that plagued both sexes.

Retro-mania filled wardrobes with flea-market sequins and feathers, while in clubs dotted across the country boys in zoot suits and girls with 1940s flicks, eyeliner and platform shoes danced to Glenn Miller.

Britain was beset by economic crisis and mounting jobless figures. The outlook was bleak and the new leader of the Conservative Party, Margaret Thatcher – 'a mother of two with a taste for nice china' – rallied her supporters with her chilling diagnosis: 'We have lived like the heirs of an estate that could not be depleted, until we awoke one morning to find the bailiffs at the door.'

It doesn't take a PhD in psychology to work out that the layers that defined fashion's mainstream look all spoke in some way about protection. The short skirts over long skirts, the cropped sleeves over wrist length, the dresses with tabards and aprons, the piling on of pattern and textures: all were like a regression into a gentler past. Meanwhile, the glittering feather-trimmed wardrobes of the disco divas were pure escapism. And fashion remained in flamboyant denial until punk exploded into the aggression of the 1980s.

In 1976, women took to wearing men's tweed jackets for day and tuxedos for the evenings, and it looked as though fashion might finally be ready to move forward. But it wasn't until 1979 that *Vogue* finally called time on 'a decade of onion dressing'.

Diane von Furstenberg's elegantly simple wrap dress is perhaps one of the rare 70s fashion icons that has stood the test of time. Below: With disco came everything that would get you noticed on the dance floor, whether it was hot pants, silver lamé, and oceans of glitters, or as here acres of snow-white fringed chiffon – Donna Summer in 1976.

THE AFGHAN COAT

The fashion item that gave the hippies a bad smell

1970

'Flower power' – attributed to the American Beat poet Allen Ginsberg – is a slogan that conjures up a powerful image of the hippies of the early 1970s. And the one wardrobe item with which the hippies are most closely associated is the malodorous Afghan coat.

The Afghan was made from sheep- or goatskin, with the fleece on the inside and the soft leather skin on the outside. The original really did not deserve the stinky reputation it later gained in the West. Sourced in Ghazni Province, between Kabul and Kandahar in Afghanistan, it was made from cured and tanned sheepskins that were then finely embroidered with silk thread.

Afghan coats first became available in the UK in the late 1960s, at Granny Takes a Trip on London's King's Road. When The Beatles bought them and wore them inside out for the cover picture of the *Magical Mystery Tour* album (1967), a craze was born. Demand spiralled, and the Afghan artisans could not keep up. A backup supply was sourced in Iran and Turkey. Coarsely embroidered and poorly cured, these imitations turned putrid in the damp British climate, and became memorable for their room-clearing smell.

Fashion in the 1970s drew inspiration from every corner of the global village. Anything that was not rooted in Western consumer culture had wardrobe potential. Ethnic garments such as kaftans and Afghan coats retained their fashion currency well into the 1970s. They became the uniform for campaigning, peace-loving and protesting hippies everywhere – whether they were manning the barricades in Paris, protecting their squatters' rights in Notting Hill or chilling at the Pilton (later, Glastonbury) Festival, which started at Worthy Farm in Somerset in 1970.

At the heart of the 70s legend of the Afghan coat is a horrible smell. Some said it smelled like something had died. Others that the pong was so strong you could smell it before you saw it. Improved curing techniques have ensured that the frequent shaggy revivals in subsequent years have been comparatively fragrant.

ALI MacGRAW

The all-American fashion heroine

Ali MacGraw's character Jenny Cavilleri, in the 1970 sob-fest *Love Story*, had a whole wardrobe of timeless classics: camel wrap coats, striped rugby scarves, satchel bags and knitted beanie hats. Overnight she became a fashion icon. Every girl in America in the early 1970s wanted to look like Ali MacGraw (1939–). 'She exemplified this great American style,' recalls Calvin Klein. 'In the beginning, there was that rich-hippie period. But it went beyond that, and her style put her among the greats: Katharine Hepburn, Jackie Onassis, C Z Guest, Babe Paley.'

Off screen, married to Steve McQueen she was one half of Hollywood's most gilded couple. With a wardrobe full of Halstons and a spot that appeared to be annually reserved for her on the Best Dressed lists, her style status was unassailable. Almost 50 years later she still inspires designers such as Micheal Kors, Ralph Lauren and Marc Jacobs.

Ali's earliest ambitions were to work in fashion, and on graduating from college she spent time as an assistant to the legendary Diana Vreeland on *Harpers Bazaar.* 'A crash course in all I did not know about fashion and the fashion world,' she remembered. Her career, she thought, would be behind the camera. As stylist for the photographer Melvin Sokolsky, Ali was mesmerized by the 'most ravishing beauties of the time,' never once confusing, 'my ability to help dress them with any possibility that I might be one of them.'

But as the 60s ended, American fashion was emerging from Paris's shadow as a force in its own right. And the women who best represented it were, in style terms, the polar opposites of the patrician Parisiennes. When she got her unexpected movie break it was Ali's own style, her bohemian preppie look, that was central to her Jenny Cavalleri character, and turned out to be the defining fashion moment of the decade.

Camel trench, pea coat, rib-knit scarf and pull-on hat, flared jeans over heels, hobo bag (all elements of Jenny Cavilleri's wardrobe in *Love Story*): Ali MacGraw's style was fetishized by fashion and coveted by women aiming to capture the elements of timeless, all-American chic.

BILL GIBB

British fashion's Celtic visionary

As the 60s faded, an unprecedented surge of talent emerged from the Royal College of Art under the aegis of Professor Janey Ironside. Alongside Ossie Clark, Anthony Price and Zandra Rhodes there was Bill Gibb, a farmer's son from Fraserburgh in Scotland.

Fashion at the time idealized the simple life where, in the hands of artisans, a new fashion look evolved in small workshops such as Missoni in Italy. The homespun became a game-changing fashion hit when Gibb met Kaffe Fassett, the American painter-turned-knitting guru (see page 62). The marriage of Gibb's Celtic romance combined with Fassett's technical skill was a defining influence on the look of the decade.

Gibb's Scottish background, his love for the historic, especially the Renaissance, and the American hippie culture introduced to him by Fassett, resulted in a collection that was pure escapism. Its hand-dyed tartans, bold checks, Gibb's painstaking re-creation of dream landscapes hand painted on to yards of fabric and Fassett's fantastical hand knits were catwalk gold, beloved by the press, if almost impossible to produce in any significant quantities.

As the sharp realities of the new decade started to bite, Gibb offered a kind of fashion fantasy through his rich embroideries and lavish layering. His signature silhouette was a billowy, ankle length, doll-like smock often embroidered or decorated, however discreetly with his motif – a little honey bee.

Bill Gibb was voted Designer Of The Year by *Vogue* in 1970 and his debut collection under his own name in 1972 had customers including Elizabeth Taylor, Bianca Jagger (see page 16) and Twiggy.

In 1971, Gibb wowed New York and became internationally famous overnight when he dressed Twiggy for her red carpet appearance for the premiere of Ken Russell's film *The Boyfriend*. His philosophy was simple: 'Reality is so horrific these days that only escapism makes it bearable at times.'

Bill Gibb grew up far from the excesses of high fashion and always remained a romantic idealist, shunning material wealth and possessions. Throughout his life, he remained much like his childhood self, the boy who 'had raided a dressing-up box to transform his sisters into miniature Rapunzels or wee Ladies of Shallot'.

SOUL TRAIN

The look of African-American soul

It was a launch pad for the giants of soul – Smokey Robinson, Aretha Franklin, Stevie Wonder, the O'Jays, Marvin Gaye, the Isley Brothers and Barry White all hitched a ride on *Soul Train*. Not only did it foster burgeoning music talent, it was the place where America tuned in to check out the hottest dance moves and coolest fashion trends. It also gave African-American music and popular culture an equal opportunity on the television airwaves.

The show's host and originator was Don Cornelius (1936–2012). With his stage swagger, his sharp suits and his smooth talking, he was the epitome of cool. The show launched in Chicago, where every week Cornelius showcased and interviewed the latest R&B acts and introduced dance numbers performed by the show's own 'Soul Train Gang'. It all took place on a club set – a format copied by music shows all over the world.

Key features were the 'Soul Train Scramble Board', where two dancers were given 60 seconds to unscramble a set of letters to reveal the name of that show's performer or of a notable person in African-American history. And then there was the 'Soul Train Line', in which the audience formed two lines with a space in the middle for dancers to strut down catwalk style.

In the beginning the show was supported by two key sponsors: Sears Roebuck and Company, which wanted to promote its record players, and Johnson Products, makers of Afro Sheen hair-care products. Cornelius became an icon of the generation not only because he was the godfather of cool, but because of his formidable commercial clout. Artists lined up to appear on *Soul Train*, as an appearance guaranteed an increase in sales and recognition.

In February 2012, fans gathered in their thousands to honour Cornelius, the recently deceased *Soul Train* creator. Donning Afros, they re-created a Soul Train Line in New York City's Times Square, which lasted almost an hour before police broke it up.

In the 1970s *Soul Train* was must-see TV – a weekly extravaganza which became a pop culture juggernaut that broke new ground for African-American entertainment. It was a launch pad not only for music talent but for the dance moves and fashion trends that took hold in the dance clubs and on the streets of America within days of their endorsement on the show.

BIANCA JAGGER
The original rock 'n' roll bride

It was unlikely that Bianca Pérez-Mora de Macias (1945–) would ever be a traditional bride. The woman who was best friends with Andy Warhol, queen of the New York nightclub scene, a pillar of the Studio 54 set and an honorary 'Halstonette' had bagged a Rolling Stone and was getting married in St Tropez. She was never going to wear a billowing meringue of taffeta. Instead she went to Yves Saint Laurent.

He wore sneakers. She wore a white tuxedo. 'I had a very clear idea of what I wanted as a wedding dress,' she said. 'Contrary to popular wisdom, it wasn't a trouser suit: it was a long, narrow skirt and a jacket. He made the wide-brimmed hat with a veil and we decided that instead of carrying a bouquet I should wear a flower corsage on my wrist to go with the suit.'

Bianca set a new standard for the modern, minimalist bride. Some of it was happenstance: she wore the jacket with nothing underneath because she was four months pregnant (with daughter Jade) and the blouse that went with her ensemble no longer fitted. Some of it was by design: the floppy-brimmed hat was perfect for shielding her not only from the St-Tropez sunshine but also from the paparazzi – there in such numbers that the ceremony had to be postponed for over an hour. Nonetheless, it was a look that has been copied on catwalks and by brides all over the world ever since.

The hat and corsage were her only bridal accessories. The civil ceremony, which took place in the town hall, had a rocky start when an argument broke out between Jagger's spokesman and local police over the number of paparazzi who had been allowed into the hall. Bianca must have been grateful for the big-brimmed hat and veil when, in a fit of pique, Jagger threatened to abandon the ceremony altogether, and made his bride cry.

He wore Tommy Nutter; she wore YSL. Her wedding look may have been designed principally to disguise her pregnancy, but she still managed to inspire a decade with her nipped-in waist, sharp-shouldered silhouette and romantic veiled hat.

GERMAINE GREER

Standard-bearer for the sexual revolution

The 1970s was the decade of women's liberation when the dolly birds of the 1960s decided enough was enough. In 1970 Germaine Greer's book *The Female Eunuch* prompted a decade of political debate. Later in the decade magazines such as *Ms* and *Spare Rib* increasingly found their way into women's homes, and the feminist publishing house Virago was launched. But in 1970 women working at the BBC still weren't allowed to wear trousers, and women were refused mortgages in their own right and required the signature of a male guarantor. In the same year, Barbara Castle as Secretary of State for Employment introduced the Equal Pay Act. It finally came into force in 1975, together with the Sex Discrimination Act.

A lecturer in English at Warwick University, the Australian-born Greer (1939–) was also an underground journalist, a singer, a dancer and an actress. She argued for revolutionary change in the social structure. Her aim was to get the message of women's liberation across, whether it meant writing about the hazards of going to bed with an Englishman who suggested 'Let's pretend you are dead' or how not to lose your temper when asked 'Do you hate men?'

When she opined that 'Bras are a ludicrous invention', it was an 'aha' moment for millions. In America, protesters encamped outside a Miss America beauty contest set up a 'Freedom Trash Can', which was filled with bras, high-heeled shoes, false eyelashes, girdles, curlers, hairspray, make-up, corsets, magazines such as *Playboy*, and other items thought to be accoutrements of 'enforced femininity'. Contrary to popular myth, no fire was lit.

The genie was out of the bottle. 'The body has become a sign of resistance,' feminists argued. And fashion, too, had become political. The new feminist ideals found expression in wardrobes that were functional, utilitarian and androgynous. The conservative Right might have railed against the 'braless, brainless broads', but throughout the decade women continued to experiment with the novelty of their new-found freedoms.

The promenent feminist Midge McKenzie described Greer as 'a phenomenon, a super heroine […] who raises the possibilities for other women. Although some of them feel there is only room for one girl who both enjoys sex and has a Ph.D.'

In *The Female Eunuch* Germaine Greer declared, 'I'm sick of pretending eternal youth…. I'm sick of peering at the world through false eyelashes… I'm sick of weighting my head with a dead mane… I'm sick of the Powder Room.' In the 70s, fashion became a central issue in the gender equality debate.

GUCCI

The Florentine artisan becomes a global luxury giant

1971

Gucci's empire sprang from the seed of an idea that was sown in the mind of the young immigrant Guccio Gucci (1881–1953), who worked as a porter at the Savoy Hotel in London. He was fascinated with the luggage owned by aristocratic guests, and had the opportunity to examine the best of it up close. In 1920 he returned to his home town, Florence, to open a shop specializing in fine leather goods made by local artisans. It took less than 50 years for the small family business to become a world-class luxury goods label, and for the instantly recognizable logo of interlocking Gs to become the insignia of the jet set in VIP airport lounges across the globe.

In the 1930s, Gucci's three sons joined the business. The exigencies of World War II (when leather was in short supply) spawned the iconic canvas bags, but by the time the economy was booming again the company was ready with those famous interlocking Gs that were to become shorthand for a new kind of chic for the swinging generation. The best of Florentine artisanal skill met the postwar economic boom with treasures to tempt the newly moneyed, such as bags with curved bamboo handles, snaffle-bit loafers, and silks printed with flowers and butterflies.

Gucci became famous, but it was when Jackie Onassis was photographed carrying the classic hobo bag that fame became a frenzy. Gucci was one of the hottest – or should that be coolest? – labels of the 1970s. A ready-to-wear collection ensured that space was found for those famous GGs on everything from baby crocodile coats to cashmere scarves.

The brand became known as much for its audacious innovation as for its peerless Italian quality and craftsmanship. In 1977 the Beverly Hills flagship store was revamped with a private Gucci Gallery, where VIPs such as Rita Hayworth and Michael Caine could browse for $10,000 bags with detachable gold and diamond chains, or for platinum-fox bed throws.

With monogrammed leather, iconic hardware such as the snaffle-bit trim, or signature stylings such as the bamboo handle on a bag, Gucci devised a new language of luxury that was instantly recognizable and coveted all over the world. In the 1950s and 60s, Gucci was a celebrity cult. In the 70s it became a global giant.

JONI MITCHELL

Songwriting siren and social commentator

A hybrid of the California beach babe, Norse goddess and coffee-bar intellectual, Joni Mitchell (1943–) reigned as the bohemian queen of the 1970s. Like most folk singers, the Canadian-born singer got her start performing in coffee shops and busking on the street. Her unique songwriting, innovative guitar style and astonishing vocal range placed her at the forefront of the folk movement.

Mitchell also defined the look of the peacenik hippie. Her iconic hairstyle of blunt fringe and free-flowing locks, scrubbed clean face, eclectic jewellery and a wardrobe featuring everything from simple girlish minidresses to floaty maxi-dresses over bare feet became the look of choice for every arts-and-crafts, guitar-playing indie girl from New York to LA. Mitchell's style influence, like her music, reaches from counterculture to mainstream celebrities such as Nicole Richie and Rachel Zoe. It resurfaces every time boho chic makes a catwalk comeback.

With war raging in Vietnam and the anti-nuclear movement gaining momentum, student strikes and peace protests galvanized America's disaffected youth. The spirit of protest – the concept of the 'voice of the people' – found expression in contemporary folk music and spawned some of the greatest songwriters ever. Mitchell's contemporaries and collaborators were Crosby Stills, Nash & Young and Bob Dylan. Folk singers were at the forefront of social campaigns. The hit single from Joni Mitchell's *Ladies of the Canyon* (1970) album was the environmental anthem 'Big Yellow Taxi'.

Joni Mitchell rose to fame performing stripped-down acoustic music that encompassed both gloomy assessments of the world around her and exuberant expressions of romantic love – all rendered with her incredible vocal range and intimate lyrics. As Emma Thompson's broken-hearted character Karen, in *Love Actually* (2003), says: 'Joni Mitchell taught your cold English wife how to feel.'

Joni Mitchell held the record-buying public's attention with her heartfelt lyrics, her melancholy take on the world around her and her florid expressions of romantic love. She became the perfect poster girl for the hippie generation.

KANSAI YAMAMOTO
Japan's first great fashion export

In 1971, aged 27, Kansai Yamamoto (1944–) became the first Japanese designer to show in London. He was in the vanguard of the wave of Japanese fashion talent who made such a deep impact on Western fashion in the 1980s. But while he may have shared his compatriots' iconoclastic approach to shaping a silhouette, his flamboyance was diametrically opposed to the cerebral minimalism.

In his flamboyant theatricality, Kansai Yamamoto pays homage to kabuki, the traditional Japanese dance-drama. His gaudy, larger-than-life intensity was much closer to being a Japanese counterpart of Western pop art than to the sober deconstructions of the designers who followed in his wake almost a decade later. He spun fashion out of fantastical images, blending a romantic vision of the past with sci-fi imaginings of a space age future. In his silhouettes, the samurai met the intergalactic warrior.

Yamamoto is most famous as the man responsible for the wardrobe for David Bowie's Ziggy Stardust Tour. Legend has it that Bowie watched a video of a rock-fashion show that Yamamoto had staged in Japan, and fell in love with the costumes. He purchased the famous 'woodlands animal costume' – a knitted playsuit in saffron yellow – from Kansai's London boutique and went on to wear it at the Rainbow Concert in August 1972. Bowie then commissioned Yamamoto to create nine costumes for the 1973 UK tour. A stand-out piece was the knitted, multi-coloured, one-legged body sock made of metallic yarn in sections of pink, red and blue with opposing patches of graphic back and white, which 'Ziggy' wore with a turquoise feather boa. And then there was the 'Space Samurai' costume, made from a glossy quilted material in black, red and blue, with legs flared in an extravagant curve.

Kansai Yamamoto products are widely licensed in Japan, and his fashion shows – the Kansai Super Shows – have been held in various international locations, including Moscow's Red Square, drawing audiences of hundreds of thousands.

Using diverse but distinctly Japanese references, from the silken kimono to samurai armour and kabuki theatre satins, Kansai Yamamoto became the 1970s' principal fashion fantasist. He forged a path into the Western market for the generation of Japanese designers who followed in his wake.

A PASSION FOR PRINT
When too much was never enough

As the 1970s dawned, *Vogue* announced, 'There are no rules in the fashion game now. You're playing it and you make up the game as you go, […] you write your own etiquette. Express yourself.' Indeed, the decade opened on a note of soft-focus fashion anarchy. There was no dominant 'look', no leading trend. On the contrary, every available element added to the vocabulary of the fashionable woman… even bad taste. In a feature in the summer of 1972, *Vogue* dedicated six pages to the question that some cynics believe defined the decade: 'Is Bad Taste a Bad Thing?'

Women were dressing for themselves. These were not clothes made to climb the career ladder. Nor did they have much sex appeal. Attracting men seemed to be of secondary importance in this wardrobe of pinafores, aprons, smocks, bare feet in clogs, faded cotton skirts, bonnets and Liberty-print blouses. Favourite fashion shoot locations seemed to be sun-dappled picnic spots under ancient oak trees. And many fashion stories could easily have doubled as maternity features. It was a great time to be pregnant.

There was an explosion of prints and designers and women were experimenting with ways to wear them. In Paris, Yves Saint Laurent styled big-collared spotted shirts with window-pane checked skirts and topped them off with patchwork-knit vests. In Italy, the Missonis worked with Spanish-shawl prints and brilliant stripes. They invited painters to experiment with effects in the factory in Milan, and adapted them for their new collections. The Missoni model of layering textures, patterns and colours was leading the way to a knitting revolution.

From the Paris catwalks to the King's Road boutiques, designers everywhere were mixing up the Liberty lawn cottons. Hand-knitters busied themselves with the production of vest tops, which were then layered over long-sleeved sweaters or shirts and blouses in patterns that might have related, but certainly did not match. Women began to think in families of colours and pattern groups when putting their looks together. The fashion rule book had been shredded.

Clashing print, clashing textures, multiple layers of fabric and a love affair with colour (a love that some would say was blind) were what *Vogue* dubbed 'onion dressing'. For many, 1970s fashion's obsession with print and colour clash explored the extreme limits of good taste.

BELL-BOTTOMS

Style crime or figure flatterer?

Flares, loons, parallels, bells, boot-cut, hip huggers and elephant bells: to the casual observer they are all flared trousers, but the difference between them all is a wealth of fabric. In the 1970s, degrees of flare ranged from the modest 6-inch boot-cut (so conservative that it has slipped into the annals of the classic wardrobe) to the elephant flare, with its absurdly wide 25 inches.

Flares first arrived as high-fashion items on the Paris couture catwalks in the 1960s, progressed to hippie counterculture status around the turn of the decade, and hit the mainstream in the 1970s. To this day there are fashion commentators who blame Sonny and Cher for flared crimes against fashion as the nationwide explosion of the trend in America appears to have gained traction just after they wore them on their prime-time television show.

Loons flared more from the knee than typical bell-bottoms, in which more of the leg was flared. They were much loved by heavy-metal rock musicians such as Led Zeppelin, who were instantly recognizable in their loons, skin-tight T-shirts and tiny jackets, accompanied, more often than not, by a matching shock of flared hair. Disco music gave flares a new lease of unisex life in glorious and often shiny Technicolor.

Elephant bells, popular in the mid-to-late 1970s, were similar to loon pants but typically made of denim. Elephant bells had a marked flare below the knee, often covering the wearer's shoes, and were consequently taken up by performers of shorter stature such as James Brown, for whom the extra inches of height were a fashion godsend.

When the decade ended, most people hoped they'd seen the back of bell-bottoms. However, they made a strong recovery in fashion circles in 2010.

For every crime against fashion that has been attributed to flared trousers, there is mitigating evidence that – given a slim enough line, a long enough leg and a high enough heel – the flared trouser is a useful weapon in the front line of the battle to lengthen legs and slim hips.

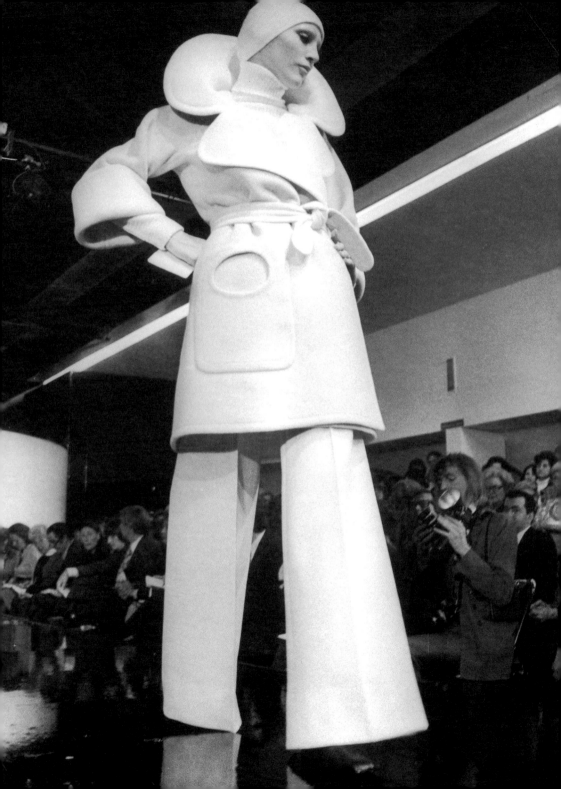

BEVERLY JOHNSON

American *Vogue*'s first black cover girl

Thanks to a single photograph in a blue polo-necked sweater, Beverly Johnson (1952–) became almost overnight a symbol of and a role model for the American Civil Rights Movement, was invited to speak by the Reverend Jesse Jackson and was name checked alongside Rosa Parks and the Black Panthers.

'Except for the birth of my daughter, my *Vogue* cover was the best thing that ever happened to me,' says Johnson. The first black supermodel was raised in Buffalo, New York, and trained as a competitive swimmer, which, she said, made her 'a model with an athlete's mindset'. But, while Johnson had graced other US magazine covers, she had never made it to the cover of *Vogue* – the gold medal in terms of modelling. Neither had Naomi Sims or Helen Williams, the two other leading African-American models of the time. But the early 1970s were a time of social upheaval, and things were about to change.

Johnson left her model agent Eileen Ford because Ford had told her she'd never get the coveted prize. 'I thought it was because I wasn't her top model,' she said, 'not because I was black.' She signed with Ford's competitor, Wilhelmina, because she assured her it was within her reach. And it was. At 22 years old, Beverly Johnson became the first African-American woman on the cover of *Vogue,* with the issue of August 1974. A year later she was also the first black model on the cover of French *Elle*. She realizes just how important that *Vogue* cover was – and not just for her modelling career: 'Black beauty had not only been acknowledged in the mainstream, but celebrated.'

'Her' issue of *Vogue* sold out: 'The magazine was changing. It wasn't so much about the grand fashion fantasy as it had been in the 60s. It was more about the girl next door.' The cover was shot by Francesco Scavullo. Johnson remembered that there weren't many photographers and make-up artists who really understood how to light women of colour. Scavullo – along with make-up artist Way Bandy and hairdresser Suga – got it.

Johnson was paid the princely sum of $100, which was the editorial day rate, but went on to become one of the highest-paid models in the industry, making about $100 per hour for advertising work.

Beverly Johnson became a 21-year-old trail-blazer as the first African-American model to appear on the cover of American *Vogue*. She repeated her triumph in August 1975, and was followed by Peggy Dillard in August 1977. Naomi Campbell was the first black model to make the cover of a big fashion issue in September 1989.

CLOGS

Utilitarian, unisex, unpretentious … and ugly?

Clogs are the one fashion item that springs immediately to mind in support of any argument that the 1970s is 'the decade that style forgot'. For shoe connoisseurs, clogs are what happen when comfort and practicality trounce fashion and style. And so, for many fashion lovers, they are a classic cautionary tale.

They are also a fascinating window into the soul of the 1970s. It was a glamorous, frivolous decade, easily caricatured for some of its more extreme trends. But it was also a turbulent and often violent decade, wracked by political scandal and economic crisis. On marches and demos throughout the decade, marginalized groups including gay men, African Americans and women fought for the right to be treated as equal.

The hippie idealists of Europe and America were naturally drawn to the Scandinavian dream. Clogs, the footwear of workers in Sweden and the Netherlands, became not only fashionable but also emblematic of enlightened political thinking. The clog channelled not only the (very trendy) Scandinavian romantic folkloric tradition, but also came with a nod to eco-sensitivity and more than a whiff of the idealistic culture of communes. Swedish sexual liberation gave clogs a daring edge, too. They might have been heavy and bulky, but at least they could be slipped on and off easily.

As people expressed their disillusion with what they saw as the rampant consumerism of the West, those hippie ideals of peace, environmentalism and democratic socialism found their way from the margins of the music festival and into the mainstream. Clogs were utilitarian, unisex, comfortable and practical. Comprising wooden soles and leather strap or top with open heels, they were considered the shoes of both the conscience-stricken fashionable woman and the avant-garde man. They are enduring examples of accessories for the politically correct.

Speaking to the organic lifestyle and the utopian ideal of gender equality (at least via unisex footwear), the clog's 'worthier than thou' image gained no lasting fashion traction and quickly dropped off the fashion radar. Frequent attempts at revivals generally haven't achieved more than novelty status.

DIANE VON FURSTENBERG WRAP DRESS

Taking over the world, one dress at a time

In 1976, Diane von Furstenberg (1946–) became the first designer to make the cover of *Newsweek* magazine, which called her the 'most marketable designer since Coco Chanel'. It had been only seven years since she had been interning in an Italian clothing factory, and she had just married Prince Egon von Furstenberg, one of Europe's most eligible bachelors. The couple had met at college. When the prince's work took them to New York, she was determined to make a career for herself. 'When I discovered I was pregnant. I was humiliated, worried people would think I'd done it to get the "best catch in Europe".'

In 1972, with a $30,000 investment and some influential friends in the fashion press (Diana Vreeland was an early supporter), she launched the Diane von Furstenberg label with a cotton jersey shirt dress and a ballerina wrap top. A couple of years later the shirt dress and top had morphed into one of fashion's all-time bestsellers – the wrap dress. And von Furstenberg was not only posing for photographs by Andy Warhol, lunching with Vreeland and appearing in the party pages of *Vogue*, she was even on the cover of the *Wall Street Journal*.

The wrap dress – sexy, simple, packable and good on women of many shapes and sizes – was an unprecedented success. By 1976, just two years after its launch, sales of the wrap dress had topped the 5 million mark. Von Furstenberg explained its instant appeal: 'The wrap dress is the most traditional form of dressing: It's like a robe, a kimono, a toga. It doesn't have buttons or zippers. What made it different was that it was jersey; it made every woman look like a feline. And that's how it happened. It's not like I was thinking "Oh, I'm creating the It dress".'

It hasn't hurt that von Furstenberg is always perfectly PR-able. When, in the 1980s, a French journalist asked her to explain how 'that dress' came about, she added another layer to the fashion legend: 'Well, if you're trying to slip out without waking a sleeping man, zips are a nightmare.'

In 1975, von Furstenberg was making 15,000 dresses a week, to be worn by everyone from suburban housewives to Betty Ford and Gloria Steinem. As von Furstenberg herself says, 'The wrap dress was an interesting cultural phenomenon, one that has lasted 30 years.'

Feel like a woman, Wear a dress!

HOT PANTS

The booming business of body awareness takes off

By the winter of 1970–1 the midi-skirt had completely ousted the mini from the catwalks, and yet designers seemed loth to abandon bare legs. They proposed instead the shortest shorts, worn either on their own or under thigh-high slit dresses or showing under transparent layers. Yves Saint Laurent reinterpreted the 1940s with hot pants and wide-lapelled blazers, and Valentino showed a thigh-split, front-fastened skirt over white shorts.

Hot pants sold like hotcakes all over Europe and North America. 'Hot pants' entered the *Oxford English Dictionary*. And James Brown immortalized 'the girl over there with the funky hot pants on.' The craze might have enjoyed catwalk limelight for less than a year, but it was a benchmark for just how radically rules of dress and behaviour had changed. In that short time, it had become socially acceptable for women to wear them on the street, to the office, even to weddings. Even Jackie Onassis wore them.

But, as often happens, a fashion craze was the superficial representation of something much more significant. As the average woman got larger, models and celebrities were becoming thinner. A new culture of starvation had arrived, and a new market for diet pills, diet drinks and diet food had been identified. Hot pants reflected a new body awareness among Western women.

When hot pants fell out of favour in the summer of 1971, only months after they first took the world by storm, some fashion writers speculated that their disappearance was due to the fact that their revealing shape 'didn't work' with 'real' women's bodies. Others proposed that sex workers had killed the trend by adopting them as their own style statement. Whatever the reason for their early demise, by 1972 hot pants were no longer hot and were relegated to the disco, where they continued to enjoy a life as an icon of the dance floor.

Hot pants were in the mainstream for a relatively short period of time. Southwest Airlines launched a business with free inflight cocktails and this advertising tag line: 'Remember What It Was Like before Southwest Airlines? You Didn't Have Hostesses in Hot Pants. Remember?' By 1976, there were no more free drinks and the hostesses were back in navy, knee-length, A-line skirts.

THE MULLET

Lord and Lady Mullet: Paul and
Linda McCartney shag the 70s

1972

In the 1970s Wings took America, and fashion's ugliest cut took hold like a global hairstyling pandemic. Throughout the decade the mullet's prevalence among England's rock 'n' roll royalty became a phenomenon, making for what one American music critic was moved to call 'a blimey brotherhood of bitchin' hair'. The mullet came to define an entire subculture, which continues to unite a disparate tribe that takes in sporting and music legends alike.

Originally there was 'the shag', which was essentially a dishevelled and unruly mane with short spiky tufts on top and shoulder-length strands down the back. A descendant of the mod haircut, it was popularized by Rod Stewart and Keith Richards, who throughout the 'flower power' era retained a cocky 'Jack the lad' attitude to go with their mod brush.

The 1970s was a dynamic period in the evolution of the mullet. There was the Midwest Metal mullet, also known as 'the Scorpion', as styled by Joe Elliot of Def Leppard. There was the Nashville mullet, or the 'Kentucky Waterfall', of which sightings were rarer, as it was generally covered by a cowboy hat. There were mullets with political significance, such as the Eastern Bloc mullet, also known as 'Prague Spring'. This style lasted all the way to the end of the 1980s and the collapse of the Berlin Wall, when the *Mulletkopf* – the German for 'mullet-head' – came to symbolize the struggle for freedom.

Soul brothers joined in with the African-American mullet, whose leading proponent was Barry White. And serious students of the hirsute need look no further than Linda McCartney for an example of the Lady mullet. The mullet, it seems, transcended boundaries of sex, nationality, politics, class and, most of all, taste.

The common link is undoubtedly Paul and Linda McCartney who were the undisputed mullet originators.

It's a dark chapter in hair-dressing history. Tom Jones is believed to have sported the first; David Bowie, the coolest. But Paul and Linda McCartney launched a trend that carries on to this day, and which at various times has gathered the likes of Suzi Quatro, Andre Agassi, Mel Gibson and Billy Ray Cyrus along the way.

DAVID AND ANGIE BOWIE

The thin white Duke and his Duchess
First couple of cool

There were John and Yoko, and Mick and Bianca, and then there were David Bowie (1947–) and Angela Barnett (1949–), the flame-haired, loud-mouthed American who inspired Bowie to develop his Ziggy Stardust, Aladdin Sane and Thin White Duke personae. David and Angie were British rock's quirky royal couple, looking and dressing alike in bright-red mullets and silk kimonos, and shocking the music world with scandalous tales of drugs, cross-dressing, threesomes and bisexual trysts.

The 1970s were characterized by sexual exploration. Terms such as homosexuality and androgyny became familiar, and it was the British glam rockers who were the flag-bearers for this sexual evolution. Glam was suddenly all the rage, on both sides of the Pond. Boys borrowed girls' boas, blouses, slinky shirts and sometimes even their make-up.

Fashion was an integral part of David Bowie's image. As big glasses were to Elton John, so sequined leotards and feather boas were to Bowie's alter ego, Ziggy Stardust. The make-up skewed the gender lines even further. He became the most outrageous performer of the decade.

Bowie and Barnett met in London in 1969, through a mutual acquaintance, or as Bowie put it, 'because we were both going out with the same man'. Angie's arrival encouraged Bowie to explore his androgynous side. She introduced Bowie to many of the arty eccentrics who would provide the blueprints for his future avatars.

The couple were married in 1970 and divorced in 1980. The decade was Bowie's most exciting period, his 'golden years'. It started with *The Man Who Sold the World* and closed with *Scary Monsters*. During this period he made 12 successful albums, all seminal landmarks in music, all unforgettable fashion moments.

She was the daughter of a US army colonel. He was an aspiring rock star. They shared a talent for outrage. 'I was wild and David needed me to help him be wild,' said Angie. 'I chopped his hair off and dyed it and put him in a dress. I gave him notoriety. He gave me fame.' Together they created some of the most memorable fashion icons of the decade.

KENZO

Taking Paris in a riot of colour

1973

The Japanese fashion invasion of Europe was led by Kenzo Takada (1939–), who proposed a completely different approach to silhouette and a radical use of texture and colour. Through him, Europe was to discover the Eastern tradition of covering the body in loose layers, rather than outlining it with a figure-hugging cut.

Kenzo was one of the first male students at Tokyo's Bunka Fashion College. In Japan at that time, traditional styles of dress dominated. The East was increasingly open to Western ideas and styles, but none of the Japanese designers had the confidence to challenge the supremacy of Paris until Kenzo arrived in the fashion capital in 1969. He rejected the untouchable image of Parisian couture, and his colourful, breezy style went off at a radical tangent to the past. In a challenge to the cold elegance of the Parisian shows, his models were lively and his presentations informal.

Kenzo found instant success with his debut for Spring 1970. Square-cut shapes reflected the ease of the kimono; unstructured clothes had a delicate sensuousness. Once asked why he didn't design sexy, close-fitting clothes, he winced and said: 'I couldn't, I'm too shy.' Through his work he channelled the vibrancy and colour he experienced on his travels, with the folklore of the Orient, Peru or India ever present. He drew on influences as disparate as calligraphy, military uniforms and ecclesiastical robes. Inspirations from the fine arts included Kandinsky and Hockney.

At the heart of Kenzo's style was a vibrant international eclecticism. Saint Laurent might have turned ethnic motifs into fashion themes but Kenzo's ideal was the harmony of many cultural influences. He chose to call his early collections 'Jap', intending thereby to take the pejorative sting out of a racist slur. His peaceful internationalism was one of his most radical contributions.

Kenzo epitomized the fashion energy and imagination of the 1970s, and his brilliance brought style and global influences to bear on Paris fashion.

Kenzo epitomized the fashion energy and imagination of the 1970s, and his brilliance brought a combination of street style and ethnic themes to bear on Paris fashion. Under his influence, fashion fell in love with globalism. It is a passion that still resonates today.

42

LAURA ASHLEY
Taking fashion back to basics

Opening her first shop in London in 1967, Laura Ashley (1925–85) specialized in the Victorian milkmaid look – dresses in sprigged cottons and white high-necked blouses which she sold at affordable prices. Ashley's clothes reflected the decade's strong anti-fashion mood as well as the back-to-nature movement that sprang from the hippie reaction to consumer-boom America and the environmental crisis that it had helped to create. The back-to-nature movement also inspired a nostalgia for a more innocent past, and embraced a Victorian fantasy of simple, homespun interiors and fashion.

'Surely you want to leave some contribution of the age we've lived in?' Laura Ashley's friend Terence Conran once needled her. Laura replied, 'I'm only interested in reopening people's eyes to what they have forgotten about.' Commentators theorized that her style was in part a feminine reaction against the sexist fashions of the 1960s. In contrast to that decade's preference for synthetics, Laura Ashley clothes were made from natural fabrics such as cotton and favoured soft floral prints.

Having tapped the nostalgic mood, Laura Ashley enjoyed rapid success and went on to construct an entire lifestyle 'landscape' around her product – a pioneering innovation at that time. By 1981 there were 5,000 outlets worldwide stocking her product. Her pin-tucked bodices, leg o' mutton sleeves and floral printed cottons reminiscent of nineteenth century china patterns were huge high street hits. In no small way the Laura Ashley ethos was a reflection of the prevailing confusion about women's roles.

Laura's acquisition of a chateau in Picardy in 1978 is widely considered a watershed moment. Commentators saw no coincidence in the subsequent hike in the prices of garments that were once affordable to many, and were now edging out of their reach. Laura herself seemed to have become increasingly out of touch and in favour of a particularly heavy cotton in her bedding collection, arguing, 'Oh, but surely everyone sends their sheets to a laundry these days?'

The back-to-nature movement sprang from a reaction to the consumer boom, and through it handcrafts such as knitting, embroidery, natural dyeing and leather tanning enjoyed a revival. Laura Ashley harnessed the power of nostalgia for a simpler life, and with it built an empire.

MARC BOLAN

The 'National Elf' becomes the poster boy for glam rock

Marc Bolan's rise was meteoric, dazzling… and brief. His career spawned an influence that ended in a fatal car crash after only 18 months of chart topping success, yet still resonates through music and fashion decades after his death.

He was the 'National Elf'; a flamboyant troubadour with a dandy wardrobe and a penchant for tall tales. At the peak of his career in the early 70s Bolan sported a tumble of girlish curls and a head-turning look that was a mixture of Biba blouses, velvet trousers from Kensington Market, the obligatory Afghan and Mary Jane button strap shoes – a style he was said to favour because his feet were exceptionally small. On paper the elements don't add up to sex symbol, but he had a charisma that appealed to both genders.

'It was like being jealous of your best girlfriend,' recalled Cilla Black who performed with him. 'He had everything – the hair, the eyes, the make-up, the glam. The worrying thing was you did kind of fancy him, being this feminine-looking guy.' To the girls, Marc Bolan was a hybrid of the fairytale prince and a rampant boogie man. The boys had respect for a babe magnet when they saw one, even though he was dressed in satin and feathers.

In March 1971 his performance of Ride a White Swan on *Top Of The Pops* became a national talking point. Parents were outraged by his sexual ambiguity. The press called it T-Rexstacy.

Clothes and storytelling had always been important to Bolan. As 14-year-old Mark Feld, he regaled *Town* magazine with a description of his expansive wardrobe including, '10 suits, 8 sports jackets, 15 pairs of slacks, 30 or 35 good shirts, 3 leather jackets, 2 suede jackets, and 30 exceptionally good ties.' Whether it was true or not it made for colourful copy and, early on, he learned the PR power behind a good yarn.

At the height of his fame, he charmed anyone who would listen with stories of how he had been befriended, in Paris, by a sorcerer; how he had sojourned in the chateau of a shaman and how he owned a 'magic cat'. It was all part of the Marc Bolan mystique that led girls and boys alike to take to the streets with tight tank tops, flapping flares and glitter glued to their faces.

The Bolan style spawned a new generation of superstars whose appeal depended as much on their image as on their music. In a decade of outrageous fashion, the glam rock style was the most outrageous of all.

DAVID BOWIE AS ZIGGY STARDUST
Ziggy and Twiggy do *Vogue*

Alter ego 'Ziggy Stardust' made David Bowie a megastar overnight. He was a torch-bearer for a generation that was disco-dancing its way into glam rock. Ziggy was a bisexual messiah: a flame-haired yob in lip gloss and mascara, silver jumpsuit and platform boots. He was a charismatic hybrid of androgynous spaceman, rent-boy Elvis and rock 'n' roll glitter queen.

Suzy Fussey was Angela Bowie's hairdresser. It was she who gave her her towering quiff and dyed it red, white and blue. Angie was so pleased with the results that she asked Fussey to work on David's hair. Between the three of them, they fashioned the iconic Ziggy look. After three days of trial and error (or should that be 'trial and terror'?) experimenting with a German dye called Red Hot Red and an anti-dandruff setting lotion called Guard, the scarlet rooster cut, with razored back and blow-dried front, was born.

The Ziggy haircut epitomized the androgyny of glam rock and was copied by both boys and girls. The Ziggy Stardust concept remains one of the most important and enduring phenomena of British youth culture. The look was reprised as recently as 2011, when Kate Moss was made over as Ziggy for the Christmas cover of French *Vogue*. Ziggy exploded onto the scene at a time of musical indulgence and sartorial apathy. He was a defiant stake in the ground in the face of advancing American cultural imperialism, while also pre-dating punk by four years.

The *Pin Ups* album cover, shot by Justin de Villeneuve (Twiggy's boyfriend and manager at the time), was originally commissioned by the editor of British *Vogue*, Bea Miller. However, de Villeneuve ended up giving the picture to Bowie to use on the album cover instead. The serene Twiggy was the perfect complement to Bowie's startled Ziggy. The album was the last of Bowie as Ziggy.

The *Pin Ups* album cover was originally commissioned for the cover of British *Vogue*. In just over a year, Ziggy Stardust had made it from being a cult figure on the margins to the very heart of popular culture. The false masks were copied by every nascent glam rocker in town, and sales from the album made Bowie the most successful artist of the year.

PLATFORM SHOES

Fashion goes for high-rise footwear

The opposing lures of nostalgia and futurism in fashion in the 1970s resulted in shoes that came with health warnings. Salvatore Ferragamo is credited with introducing the platform shoe in the late 1930s, an innovative move that typified the dynamic modernizing mood between the world wars. The romantic nostalgia of the 1970s sent stylists, fashion editors, photographers, designers and fashionable women back to a 40-year-old dressing-up box for inspiration, and the scene for a platform revival was set.

Simultaneously, these sculpted accessories became a wardrobe staple for glam rockers (who performed in them), Pop artists (who decorated them) and futuristic fantasists such as Ziggy Stardust (who built their entire image around them). But if platform shoes started on the margins, they went mainstream with startling speed. Quiz anyone about the dominant trends of the decade and most people would say flared trousers and platforms.

Designers such as Terry de Havilland – whose London shop Cobblers to the World became a place often visited by rock stars and celebrities – sold wedge shoes with ankle straps in peach, yellow, pistachio and blue snakeskin, and thigh-high, satin-lined black-leather boots. He made Tim Curry's platforms for *The Rocky Horror Show* and shoes to order for Bianca Jagger and David and Angela Bowie.

By the end of the decade nothing was too much: not the exaggerated bulgy toes, the flaring heels, nor the outrageously curvaceous soles. 'Paint your own platforms' got full-page features in *Vogue*, and colourful metallic piecing, patchwork and embroidery became run of the mill.

Platform shoes started in the early 1970s with a relatively slim sole, a modest inch. By the end of the decade, a two-inch sole and a five-inch heel were quite ordinary. The crossover from the world of fashion into rock music ensured they were more than a flash in the pan.

LAGERFELD FOR CHLOÉ

Catapulting Chloé into the forefront
of French ready-to-wear

Karl Lagerfeld (1933–) arrived at Chloé in the mid-1960s, at the peak of that decade's nostalgic revivalism. He had a passion for art deco, and the echoes of Beardsley and Klimt in his early collections perfectly captured the romantic mood. For Chloé he envisioned a floaty, almost ethereal femininity that remains at the heart of the label. His whimsical prints and fluid shapes were a sophisticated take on the ubiquitous bohemian, and made it one of the most successful collections of the decade.

The company's founder, Gaby Aghion, had started Chloé in 1952 with the intention of offering something completely different from the couture salon. Hers was to be 'luxury prêt-à-porter' – wearable yet beautiful daywear. The Chloé ateliers were equal to anything the couture houses had to offer, but they could deliver their collections off the rack, not as one-offs made to order. The spirit of Aghion's clothes had won legions of fans among fashionable young women. She had taken it a long way from the stiff formality of the chic Parisienne wardrobe in the early 50s.

Before Lagerfeld's arrival the business had faltered. He was tasked with reviving the ailing house and he did it by acknowledging a need for clothes that were languid and laid back, but with unmistakable French chic. Its bohemian, feminine detailing attracted clients such as Grace Kelly, Brigitte Bardot and Jackie Onassis.

Lagerfeld implicitly understood the spirit of the house, and adhered to the supple femininity for which Chloé was renowned. But he was also fearless in the design room. The house style remained firmly focused on pared-down sheath dresses that hovered around the figure with minimal decoration. But he also employed the embroidery skills of François Lesage to create show-stopping *trompe-l'œil* evening dresses, and he did not hesitate to take inspiration from sources that were decidedly not very Chloé at all: Carmen Miranda, for example, who provided an energizing jolt of bra top and scarf shawl among the tea dresses and cloche hats.

Karl Lagerfeld with a model wearing a dress from his Spring 1974 collection for Chloé. Under Lagerfeld's guidance, Chloé went from 'luxury prêt-à-porter' to something more widely accessible, in line with the pluralistic ethos of the 1970s. At Chloé, experimentation with myriad reference points became the designer's trademark. The fragrance Lagerfeld launched for the house in 1974 was an immediate commercial success, and Chloé continues to be one of the world's bestselling perfumes.

LAUREN HUTTON
'The greatest mannequin in history'

In 1974 Lauren Hutton (1943–) was the highest-paid model of the day, earning $200,000 a year as the Charles Revson Ultima II girl. The staggering fees that she commanded as the face of the beauty brand marked the turning point when fashion modelling became big business.

She had had a shaky start in the 1960s. Florida-born, Hutton went to New York aged 20 to seek fame and fortune. She was a $50-a-week house model for Dior, having been rejected by every agency before Eileen Ford took her up and advised her to fix her 'banana-shaped nose and gap teeth'. She had a commercial look compared to the typical fashion stars of the time – Twiggy, Tree and Veruschka. In 1966 Diana Vreeland picked her out from a line-up of 'run-throughs' because she had 'presence' and sent her to Richard Avedon, who at first rejected her as 'just another pretty face'. Hutton remembered that she worked with him 'only when the stars were out of town'.

Full stardom flourished only when the 1971 recession and the midi-skirt arrived. Suddenly, fantasies were de trop and haughty mannequins no longer sold a casual trouser suit. From 1972, Hutton posed almost exclusively for Richard Avedon and the pair dominated the pages of *Vogue*.

Newsweek said, 'When haughty elegance was in, she kept her funny flaws. When distant deadpan was de rigueur, she posed smiling and laughing. When statuesque poses studded fashion magazines, she jumped and galloped across the page.' Hutton had a naturalness that was an antidote to the glittering excess of the 1970s. Avedon called her 'the link between the dream and the drugstore. She's the girl next door but she moved away.'

Described by fashion designer Halston as 'the greatest mannequin in history', Hutton easily made the transition from modelling to movies with *The Gambler* (1974), alongside James Caan, and *American Gigolo* (1980), starring Richard Gere. Her signature style, to this day, is effortless masculine tailoring. 'Fashion is what you are offered and style is what you choose,' she once astutely observed.

Fresh-faced, gap-toothed and tousle-haired, she was dubbed 'the million-dollar girl next door'. Hutton wisely ignored the advice of fashion experts and kept her 'imperfections'. And even though *Vogue* once wrote of her that 'her nose flies west, her mouth flies north', the magazine put her on its cover no fewer than 28 times.

BARBARA HULANICKI AND BIBA
Revivalism with a straight face

In the years up to the store's spectacular crash in 1975, Biba and its founder, the Warsaw-born fashion designer Barbara Hulanicki (1936–), played a central part in making London swing. The business was ten years old when Big Biba opened in 1974 in the building that had formerly housed the Derry & Toms department store on Kensington High Street.

The Aubrey Beardsley exhibition at the V&A in 1966 had been a tipping point in the evolution of London style. Hulanicki found the Victorian illustrator's style 'bewitching and a trifle decadent', and used it as a major inspiration as she pioneered a contemporary style that blended art nouveau, art deco, Victoriana and Hollywood. The Beatles' *Sgt. Pepper's Lonely Hearts Club Band* (1967) album cover was an ironic nostalgia trip. Hulanicki's foray into Victoriana, however, was unabashed escapism: revivalism with a straight face. Hers was a love of a style that had been unfashionable for too long.

People flocked to Biba's exotic interior, with its jumble of clothes, feathers, beads and Lurex that spilled out over the counters like treasures in a cave. Thousands visited the store every week. Twiggy recalled: 'If you didn't buy what you wanted there […] it wasn't worth coming back next week and hoping it would still be there.' It attracted the 'beautiful people' like moths to a flame. And Hulanicki revelled in finessing every aspect of this perfect world. In her memoirs, she remembers how 'the postwar babies […] grew into beautiful skinny people. A designer's dream. Our skinny sleeves were so tight they hindered circulation.'

There was a record department with listening booths, a bookstall, a kasbah area overflowing with North African products, menswear, womenswear, a mistress room with negligees and edible underwear, and even a storyteller for the kids shopping with their mothers on a Saturday. There was a food hall in the basement, and the Rainbow Room restaurant was open until 2 a.m. The store hosted gigs by everyone from the New York Dolls to Liberace.

Hulanicki created the concept of shopping as an experience, a leisure activity, a social event.

Barbara Hulanicki, founder of Biba, pictured with her husband Stephen Fitz-Simon. Biba became a potent cult that is cherished to this day, even by those who never experienced it first-hand. The store was, according to *The Times*, 'an extraordinary creation, dominated by the personality of just one woman'.

HELMUT NEWTON
Master of the compelling and perverse

A particular photograph of a woman in *Vogue* caused a massive stir in the 1970s. She was dressed in a pretty summer print, lounging legs apart, and – in a provocative reversal of roles – was eyeing up a passing man. The photographer was the German-born Australian Helmut Newton (1920–2004). Provocation was at the core of his work. Behind the image of the model in the pretty Calvin Klein summer dress was a combination of qualities that readers were not accustomed to finding on a glossy fashion page. Unease? Certainly. Menace? Perhaps.

Photographers of the 1970s faced challenges that their predecessors had not. They could no longer rely on the drama and theatricality of the clothes themselves, but had to find a way to make the reader stop and look at the girl, almost despite her laid-back wardrobe. Inspired by the novels of Chandler and Spillane, Newton preferred to shoot in the street or 'real' interiors, rather than in the studio. He set up controversial scenarios – often involving the trappings of the bored and the rich – used bold lighting, and constructed striking compositions. Sexual fantasy rather than the reality of fashion was his powerful way of communicating. Via his work, porno chic became part of the fashion lexicon.

His models were cool, chic and maybe a little corrupt. He portrayed Amazonian women who, waking or sleeping, were rarely without immaculate make-up, jewellery and vertiginous heels. His models were towering incarnations of the blonde Prussian housemaids whom he remembered from his childhood in a wealthy household. The men in his photos typically appeared in submissive roles, as waiters, chauffeurs or mere onlookers. He shot some of his most famous images for Yves Saint Laurent, whose penchant for tight, wide-shouldered suits and powerful models inspired him.

Helmut's work mirrored the sexual revolution of the 1960s and 1970s, although to many feminists he was the Antichrist. He did nothing to assuage their antipathy with such blithely 'incorrect' comments as, 'Under certain conditions, every woman is available for love or something if paid …'

Helmut Newton captured the nuances of the feminist revolution, making women appear as sex objects, yet in control. Here, in an image for Calvin Klein, a fully clothed Lisa Taylor channelled the sexual revolution, sitting wide-legged while checking out the passing talent: archetypal male behaviour, not that of ladies in floral dresses.

DEBBIE HARRY
Queen of the New Wave scene

1975

Debbie Harry (1945–) was the queen of New York's New Wave scene in the 1970s: a punk Marilyn Monroe sharing the bill at CBGBs in the Bowery along with the Ramones, Patti Smith and Television. She was already over 30 when Blondie became successful (a dinosaur in punk terms), but Harry's cool, understated sexuality and two-tone blonde hair made her an instant success in pop culture.

In England and America, at the beginning of the decade, the anti-Establishment torch was passed from peace-loving hippies to defiant and anarchic punks. Nothing made either group angrier than designer clothes and disco. Like the hippies before them, the punks set themselves apart from consumer society with homemade clothes, though theirs were dark and tight fitting and their attitude scornful and wary to match. By the mid-1970s, however, elements of punk rock and fashion had evolved further into a more pop-oriented, less 'dangerous' style on both sides of the Atlantic.

Enter Debbie Harry, Andy Warhol's favourite pop star and New Wave's poster girl. Her look was inspired partly by Marilyn Monroe, but her attitude was more downtown. She might have started out as a *Playboy* Bunny Girl, but her figure had none of the voluptuous Marilyn curves. As Blondie's frontwoman, Harry went on to gain style icon status for her wardrobe of thrift-store finds and DayGlo stage outfits masterminded by designer Stephen Sprouse.

Thanks to Sprouse, published images of her look were well known before her music, ensuring instant recognition as soon as she started recording and performing. She later said: 'Stephen would find things for me to wear or go through my collection of rags and put them together. He had all that experience at Halston creating collections. He really knew what he was doing.'

Harry's look was in large part a styling triumph for designer Stephen Sprouse. 'The counterculture look was a throwback to the Mod thing,' she recalled. 'It was all in vintage stores. We coupled that with torn-up stuff we'd find on the street. Stephen made me feel confident and beautiful.'

KAFFE FASSETT

A one-man knitting revolution

In 1964 the American-born Kaffe Fassett (1937–) joined the great tide of British talent who were making London a fashion capital. With innovative designs and techniques, he introduced a tapestry-like pattern and colour to knitwear which became central to the romantic look that defined the close of the decade.

Having studied fine art in Boston, Fassett moved to England at the age of 27. Once he arrived, he remembered: 'A three-month holiday turned into an indefinite stay […] It was England that turned me from an easel painter into a fibre artist.' The timing for his personal transformation couldn't have been more perfect. An explosion of creative energy in the decade linked together many of the visual arts. When Fassett's painterly eye was applied to knitting it turned what had been a fireside skill into an art form.

On a trip to Scotland, Fassett bought 20 skeins of Shetland wool in an effort to capture the mesmerizing colours of the landscape. On the train back to London a fellow passenger taught him how to knit. His first designs appeared in 1969 as a full-page spread in *Vogue Knitting* magazine. Before long he was designing for Bill Gibb and Missoni of Italy. 'I think knitting is just incredibly magic,' he says. 'I mean who would ever think that you could just take two sticks and rub them together with a bit of thread in between and out would come this incredible tapestry of colour?'

By avoiding complicated stitches at all costs, Fassett claims to have arrived at 'non-angst knitting': 'I wanted to make it elegant so there was no point in trying anything fancy which immediately goes wrong when you drop a stitch. If you make a mistake according to my method, it can be a positive benefit.' He works with as many as 150 colours in a single garment – 'anything worth doing is worth overdoing,' he says.

Kaffe Fassett turned a simple process into an art form. With designer Bill Gibb he explored machine knitting for a while, but quickly rejected it for his favourite method: sitting barefoot and cross-legged and working intuitively with circular needles.

MARGARET THATCHER

The times they are a-changin'

In 1975 the Tories chose their first woman leader. Political commentator Ferdinand Mount said at the time: 'Mrs Thatcher has achieved something which Mrs Pankhurst would scarcely have dreamed possible – that just over 50 years after women gained the vote, a woman Prime Minister would be treated as nothing much out of the ordinary.' The MP for Finchley rejected any cause for great celebrations, saying: 'Good heavens, no. There's far too much work to be done.' Instead, the chronically able 'Mrs T' put in a brief appearance at a party in Pimlico before having a working dinner with Conservative Chief Whip, Humphrey Atkins, at Westminster. In 1979 she went on to win the general election to become the first female prime minister in the UK.

Over the decade, the world witnessed her evolution from suburban housewife to one of the most powerful women in the world. With her 'power-dressing' suits, brooch on her left lapel, pearls and boxy handbags, her style was instantly recognizable. With her Asprey bag, Tomasz Starzewski evening dresses and Aquascutum suits, she fashioned herself as the 'Iron Lady'.

An avid fan of the pussycat bow, Thatcher had countless blouses, both printed and plain, with long ties. 'I often wear bows; they are rather softening, they are rather pretty,' she said once. It was once suggested by an image adviser that Thatcher should give up her pearls, which had been given to her by her husband Dennis when their twins were born in 1953. She refused and they became part of her signature style.

Thatcher once described her handbag as the only safe place in Downing Street, and it became a symbol of her style of government.

'Margaret was very intelligent about her image, says *The Iron Lady* (2011) costume designer, Consolata Boyle. 'She made herself look more efficient, more businesslike, but always with that underlying feminine touch. She very knowingly used her feminine powers as a woman among men.'

AGNÈS B.
Fashion with a democratic accent

Agnès Andrée Marguerite Troublé (1941–) – known simply as agnès b. – quietly grew her simple designs into an international brand, and has become one of the richest self-made women in France.

Many of her original pieces remain part of her collection today: cardigans with pearl snaps, striped shirts made from the same hard-wearing cotton that rugby teams use for their shirts, and a leather jacket inspired by a portrait by the French impressionist painter Édouard Manet. Other things have changed. Few, for example, miss the notorious communal changing rooms, though the original idea was an idealistic one: 'I thought it was interesting to encourage this relationship between the customers, so that they would be talking to each other.'

A freelance designer, agnès b decided to open her own shop in the retail wasteland of Les Halles in 1976. Birds flew free in the cavernous space, built nests and hatched their chicks in the displays. 'It was very cool,' she says. 'We were writing on the walls.' Biographer Penelope Rowlands remembers: 'It was like going to Biba in London. I mean, you knew you were at the centre of the world somehow.' The environment was revolutionary and so was the product. Agnès recalls: 'I got back to designs that don't belong to anybody, like jeans – no one knows who designed jeans – plasterer jackets that we would dye in pink and red, waiters' jackets, herringbone painters' trousers. We made petticoats that we dyed ourselves in the bath. People would buy them still dripping wet.'

For a designer who had marched in the Paris student demonstrations of 1968 it was also subtly political: workers' clothes for everyone; fashion with a democratic accent; *liberté*, *égalité*, *fraternité*. Agnès b. remains an idealist. The company has never advertised because she thinks advertising is immoral, and her clothes are all made in France to avoid using exploited labour.

Agnès designs, she has often said, 'for people who have more important things to do than shop till they drop'. Agnès b. is a fashion tycoon, whose engagement with social issues has been matched only by her dedication to building a business. A diehard idealist, it is said she has never known how much money she makes.

BRYAN FERRY
AND JERRY HALL
Britain's coolest couple

1976

They were London's coolest couple. Bryan Ferry (1945–), 'the Electric Lounge Lizard', had global cred thanks to his songwriting partnership with Brian Eno in Roxy Music, his Antony Price suits, his connoisseurship of style and his refined taste for all the good things in life ('Roxy Music were more likely to redecorate a hotel room than trash it,' as one journalist quipped). Jerry Hall (1956–) was a rising fashion star and was to become one of the hottest models of the decade. She grew up in Mesquite, Texas, with ambitions to be glamorous. 'My mother and my sisters – five girls – were crazy about glamour and Hollywood movies. I styled myself on Veronica Lake and Marlene Dietrich.'

They met when Jerry was booked to appear as a mermaid on the cover of Roxy Music's 1975 album *Siren*. Legend has it that the blue paint they covered her in wouldn't come off, so Bryan offered to take her back to his house, claiming he would help her remove it (he had trained as an artist after all). They started an affair and she moved into his Holland Park home. Five months later they were engaged. He was 30, she was 19.

Hall might have been an established model when the couple met, but the *Siren* album cover propelled her to international celebrity. They were invited everywhere, including to dinner by Mick Jagger. This last engagement was to be the end of a dazzling affair. Hall left Ferry for Jagger in 1977: 'Bryan was flattered by Mick's attention, but he could also see that Mick was smitten with me. It couldn't have been nice for him.'

Jerry Hall is posing for a magazine shoot with Bryan Ferry in the Amstel Hotel in Amsterdam. Hall and Ferry had been going out for over a year and were engaged at the time. But within months she had left Ferry for Mick Jagger.

CHARLIE'S ANGELS

Crime-fighting sirens of the small screen

TV shows were a huge influence on fashion in the 1970s, and *Charlie's Angels* (1976–81) was one of the most successful. It was also one of the first to showcase women in roles traditionally reserved for men.

Kelly (Jaclyn Smith), Jill (Farrah Fawcett-Major) and Sabrina (Kate Jackson) left their boring jobs with the police to work for the Townsend Detective Agency. They were strong and independent women who fought the baddies and rescued the innocent.

Sexual politics aside, the wardrobe created a lasting impression: the skinny, masculine-tailored suits with wide lapels, open-necked shirts and form-fitting waistcoats; the high-waisted, wide-leg jeans and platform shoes – never mind the car phones in the convertibles. They are consistently name-checked as inspiration by designers whenever a 1970s revival rolls round. From Phoebe Philo to Tommy Hilfiger, *Charlie's Angels* is never far from designers' mood board when the there is a feeling for the go-getting 70s' sex symbol in the air.

And then there was the hair. The 'Farrah Flick' became one of the most wanted celebrity 'dos'. By the mid-1970s women had been freed from the tyranny of rollers by the blowdryer and curling tongs, whose versatility and portability launched a whole new approach to hairstyling. Farrah Fawcett-Major's feathered blonde hair remained the most copied style ever (until the 'Rachel cut' came along to offer some serious competition in the 1990s), and her influence on style and fashion far outlasted the relatively brief time she spent on that iconic TV show.

As the tomboy of the group, Fawcett-Major often wore a pair of Nike running shoes with her jeans thereby kick-starting the athletic trend. And the famous poster image of the actress in a swimsuit, head tilted back and grinning broadly, sold more than 12 million copies worldwide.

Jaclyn Smith, one of the original Angels, remembered, 'It wasn't meant to be Shakespeare. It was total escapism. I think young girls identified with us because we were emotionally independent, financially independent and we were role models.'

FIORUCCI
The daytime Studio 54

1976

Long before the concept of lifestyle became shorthand for the way fashion could reach the remotest corners of our lives, there was Fiorucci in Piazza San Babila, Milan, and its sister store nearby on the Via Torino. Young, hip Milanese went there for everything from jeans to gadgets, fast food and accessories. More importantly, it was a place to hang out. People met for 'five o'clock tea' and to browse the shop's antique market for vintage finds. The logo was based on a Victorian image of two little angels.

London got its first Fiorucci on the King's Road in 1975. And in 1976 it landed in New York next to Bloomingdale's. America fell in love with the magic of Italian styling. It became known as 'the daytime Studio 54', where many of the night time revellers spent their daylight hours dissecting their exploits of the night before and planning their next evening's exploits over inky espressos at the Fiorucci coffee bar. The Italian architect and founder of the Memphis Group Ettore Sottsass designed the interiors. Andy Warhol held the party launch for *Interview* magazine there. Everyone from European royalty to Jackie Onassis, Cher and Elizabeth Taylor shopped there; Truman Capote signed books in the window; and the performance artist Joey Arias worked there as an assistant alongside Christopher Ciccone, Madonna's brother. Years later Arias still had fond memories of the slippery floors: 'perfect for sliding across to catch shoplifters.'

There was even a Fiorucci car (an orange-and-blue Giulietta), which you could drive wearing your Fiorucci sunglasses (a designer first for the brand). In 1979, excitement about the opening of a shop in Beverly Hills was such that police had to assist with crowd control.

Fiorucci is credited with launching crazes for everything from designer jeans and sunglasses to parachute-cloth jumpsuits, leopard print and handbags made from workmen's metal lunchboxes. They were all icons of the disco age.

GLORIA VANDERBILT

Harnessing the selling power of celebrity

The 1970s were a golden age for denim: dungarees, bib-and-brace overalls, bell-bottoms and flares. It was the decade when denim became glamorous – a blank canvas to be painted, embroidered, fringed, frayed, studded and patched. Denim became a way to polish up a fusty image and didn't stop at clothing alone. In 1973 the Volkswagen Beetle was offered with denim seats and marketed as the Jeans Bug.

Gloria Vanderbilt (1924–) was a New York socialite and scion of one of America's oldest families. In 1976 the Indian designer Mohan Murjani proposed launching a line of designer jeans carrying Vanderbilt's name embossed in script on the back pocket, together with her swan logo. Although Calvin Klein is generally credited with the first breakthrough into what was to become the massive designer jeans market, it was Vanderbilt who took jeans a notch higher by harnessing the selling power of celebrity. By adding the lustre of her upper-class name and ritzy provenance to blue denim jeans, the venture became a global success. She was also one of the first designers to make public appearances.

Until the mid-1970s, the only blue jeans anyone really wore were made by Levi's, Lee or Wrangler. Gloria Vanderbilt jeans were designed exclusively to fit the contours of a woman's body and are cited as being the world's first designer jeans for women. Her jeans were also more tightly fitted than other jeans at the time.

Denim crossed the counterculture barrier and graduated to high-status garment, whether in Rodeo Drive or St-Tropez. Big designers from Ralph Lauren in New York to Giorgio Armani in Milan followed Vanderbilt's marketing lead. In the late 1970s, at the height of the brand's success, she was selling 10 million pairs of jeans a year.

Gloria Vanderbilt's jeans were the day-to-night staple of the disco era. She used her social A-list status to load her label with fashion kudos. And she scored cool points by casting Debbie Harry of Blondie in her TV advertising campaign.

MARIE OSMOND
The decade's peachy keen teen heartthrob

The 1970s were a vintage decade for teen idols – Shaun Cassidy, Leif Garrett and the Bay City Rollers among them. But for millions around the world, posters of Marie Osmond and her brother Donny claimed more bedroom wall acreage than any other. The *Donny & Marie* show (1976–81) was 'appointment television', broadcast in more than 17 different languages.

Marie Osmond was the only girl on the teen scene. She had success as a solo country music artist in the 1970s, covering the country pop ballad 'Paper Roses'. She was only 12 and made history as the youngest female artist to have her debut record go to number one in the charts. And she followed it up with a Grammy nomination.

Marie became the youngest-ever host of a national television variety show. And for five years, flush with pocket money to spend, she was a monumental trendsetter. The long, billowy smocks, the cherries tucked behind an ear framed with a blow-dried flick: this was a look that dominated the school discos of the decade. And as her teenage years advanced, many discovered in her wake the limitless potential of heated rollers. Osmond's appeal was such that she was immortalized in the first-ever celebrity fashion doll.

The Osmonds were wholesome, toothsome role models – sanitized sex symbols for teenagers in a world were taboos were, frankly, taboo.

Marie was slated for the role of Sandy in *Grease* (1978). She turned it down because she did not approve of the film's moral content. All the same, her hairstyle was the most requested look in salons across the world for the best part of a decade.

SONIA RYKIEL
French fashion's queen of knit

1976

In the 1960s, Sonia Rykiel (1930–) was dubbed 'the queen of knits' by her American fans. She was the most important of the women designers who emerged in France in that decade. The clothes that she designed for her husband's boutique, Laura, were hits with even the trendiest British mods.

In the early 1970s she pioneered clothes with exposed seams and no hems or linings. Well ahead of the Japanese and Belgians in exploring deconstruction and minimalism, she commented in *Women's Wear Daily*, 'people said making clothes inside out was not proper. I disagreed, because clothes that are inside out are as beautiful as a cathedral.'

Rykiel admitted that her femininity was at once one of her greatest qualifications and limitations as a designer. 'A man is sometimes more creative than a woman [designer] because he will not wear the clothes himself. Practical considerations to him are secondary. Women designers define things with a more practical eye because of the limitations of their body.'

Untrained, she began her career in fashion in 1962 'by accident' because she was pregnant and wanted a beautiful maternity dress. Success, however, came quickly – by 1967 Marylou Luther of the *Los Angeles Times* could write: 'Couture is not enough. You need a Rykiel.' Her major breakthrough, though, came in the 1970s, when her soft knitted separates embodied a style that was both liberated and sophisticated, and which struck a chord with the modern generation of working women.

'When I was little I hated clothes,' Rykiel has said. 'I only liked the same old skirt and pullover. It was war between me and my mother.' One day, as an act of rebellion, she went out naked. Maybe it's no surprise that the little girl who always liked to wear the same old sweater grew up to design fluid knits whose form changed only gradually, and clothes that were as comfortable as a second skin.

Rykiel's fans loved her for her uniquely feminine approach. In 1970, a poll of French women voted her one of the most sensuous women in the world. Rykiel's look offered a fresh alternative to formal French wardrobes.

Wonder Woman (1976–9), starring Lynda Carter, was must-see TV for the latter half of the decade. The super heroine and her alter ego, Diana Prince, were icons of feminine strength. Immediate fashion fallout was the rise in popularity of knee-high boots, which the most adventurous wore with hot pants, though most were happy to style them with a miniskirt.

Created in 1942 as part of the DC comic series, *Wonder Woman* was the brainchild of Dr William Moulton Marston, a psychologist and feminist. In the vanguard of pro-feminist thinking, Marston wanted to create a female comic character who was just as powerful as her male counterparts, without a hint of the 'damsel in distress'. Her powers included a Lasso of Truth and bullet-repelling bracelets, powers she would lose if her wrists were bound together. An Amazonian princess, Diana originally came to the West to fight the threat of Nazism. But she was a more-than-welcome visitor in the 1970s, a decade marked by fear of nuclear war and paranoia about communist plots.

A propaganda vehicle in star-spangled hot pants? Probably. But she also most definitely reflected the new craze for the body beautiful, and the rapidly expanding market in aerobics and dance classes that popularized the leotard.

Wonder Woman always triumphed over the men who stood against her. Inevitably, her ample chest, thighs of steel and gold-plated headband also made her sex-symbol status material. But the 1970s embraced her as a feminist heroine.

As America celebrated its Bicentennial, the central character of the prime-time hit *Wonder Woman*, broadcast the same year, was suitably dressed in patriotic emblems. Her stars-and-stripes costume with its golden belt of power, bullet-deflecting bracelets and unbreakable golden Lasso of Truth, is still a Halloween and costume party bestseller.

YVES SAINT LAURENT: THE RUSSIAN COLLECTION

1976–7

Paris couture fights back

The 1970s found haute couture at a crossroads. For the first time its relevance was hotly debated. The centre of 1960s social life had switched from the aristocracy to the new meritocracy. Ready-to-wear designers dictated a new pace in fashion. And the best-dressed women were shopping for more informal wardrobes that were in step with the decade's increasingly casual dress codes.

Yves Saint Laurent was pursuing a clear goal with his collection of Winter 1976/7, his most expensive and lavish collection yet. 'It was my answer to the press which had disqualified the haute couture trade as old fashioned and antiquated,' he said. With the collection, he made yet another lasting impact on fashion. His sable-trimmed Cossack coats in gold lamé, bright babushka dresses, gypsy skirts piped in gold, luxuriously embroidered waistcoats and tunics, whisper-thin glittering blouses with full sleeves, and golden Cossack boots set a new standard in luxury that was to reverberate into the 1980s.

'A revolution,' cheered the *International Herald Tribune*, 'the most dramatic and expensive show ever seen in Paris.' The press dubbed it the 'Ballets Russes' collection, in homage to Serge Diaghilev's Russian ballet troupe which had caused a similar sensation in Paris at the beginning of the century. And indeed there were distinct echoes of Leon Bakst, the company's unforgettable costume designer.

Each look was a celebration of the skills of the artisans who had contributed to it – the embroiderers, passementerie makers, lace weavers, feather workers and jewellery makers. He may be the designer who will be remembered for having made the greatest effort with his Rive Gauche label to connect with the women in their every day wardrobes and their life on the street. But with this one collection he created a distinct distance between the couture and the ready-to-wear, and revived the taste for elegant excess. 'I don't know if it's my best collection, but it was certainly my most beautiful,' the designer later recalled.

With the Russian collection, Saint Laurent not only convinced the press of the artistic worth of luxury fashion; he also brought fantasy and romance back to the catwalk and triggered a folklore wave that has never completely subsided since.

DEBORAH TURBEVILLE

Fashion photography's incurable romantic

1977

One of the most significant changes in fashion in the 1970s was the increasing numbers of influential women photographers. The prominence of the likes of Deborah Turbeville, Louise Dahl-Wolfe, Andrea Blanch, Eve Arnold and Sarah Moon reflected not only how women's place in society was changing, but also how women were perceiving other women and themselves. Men photographing women in the 1970s often presented them as something only to be desired. Women photographers tended to photograph fashion and women in a way that corresponded to their own realities, often producing images that draw strength from mood and atmosphere rather than the impact of a graphic image on the page.

The American Deborah Turbeville (1938–) was one of the most original and imitated of this new breed. As she put it, 'I am totally different from photographers like Newton and Bourdin. Their exciting and brilliant photographs put women down. They look pushed around in a hard way: totally vulnerable. For me there is no sensitivity in that. It is the psychological tone and mood that I work for.'

For inspiration Turbeville drew on 'silent films by Eisenstein, cinematic work of Cocteau, Diaghilev's ballet set drawings, Russian literature, and the faded palaces of Europe'. There is a psychological tension in Turbeville's work that reflects a preoccupation with cinematic style and atmosphere.

Turbeville shows women who desire something more than men can give. Simple daylight gives her images an enigmatic quality. Her women look delicate and even a little sinister as they gather in slightly odd environments, in faded ballrooms or wild gardens. Their oblique glances have a mysterious quality, and sometimes they look isolated or disturbed. Their surroundings are dreamlike and insubstantial. Their bodies say one thing and their clothes another. In the 1970s these ambivalences engaged many women in a powerful way.

Turbeville was (and remains to this day) hugely inspired by imagery from paintings, literature and architecture of the past. Her images were a lightning rod for the romance and nostalgia that inspired much of the fashion design of the decade.

DIANE KEATON
IN *ANNIE HALL*

The movie that spawned an enduring fashion look

Only a handful of movies can claim to have spawned an entire fashion movement. In the 1970s, women everywhere took on Diane Keaton's *Annie Hall* look, layering oversized, mannish blazers over waistcoats and ties, billowy trousers or long skirts, and donning boots.

One of Woody Allen's most taxing dilemmas on the movie was Annie's wardrobe. Her character was that of a complicated, neurotic, intelligent ditz. And what she wore had to make that believable. While Ralph Lauren and costume designer Ruth Morley collaborated on the styling, it was Keaton who created the look using her own clothes. 'She came in,' Allen recalled in 1992, 'and Ruth Morley said, "Tell her not to wear that. She can't wear that. It's so crazy." And I said, "Leave her. She's a genius."' Keaton's gender-bending wardrobe blazed a trail for women in the late 1970s.

After the release and subsequent popularity of the film, the 'Annie Hall look' became standard attire for smart girls everywhere. Those grandfather shirts, baggy chinos, Ralph Lauren ties, big hats, flat shoes and glasses became code for the female intellectual. The clothes weren't just about the right to equality; they were also about the right to individuality. Annie Hall saw the birth of vintage chic.

'Her throwaway verbal style and her thrown-together dress style became symbols of the free, friendly, gracefully puzzled young women who were busy creating identities out of the epic miscellany of materials swirling in the American cultural centrifuge,' rhapsodized Jack Kroll, *Newsweek*'s film critic at the time. 'Her fashion influence in those days should not be underestimated,' says *Vogue* editor André Leon Talley, 'What Sarah Jessica Parker is to young women today, Diane Keaton was in that day.'

The 'Annie Hall look' became a global fashion phenomenon. In the syndicated *Doonesbury* comic strip, a radio interviewer asked a fictional Iranian revolutionary leader if the Ayatollah Khomeini would approve of the look for Iranian women. The response was: 'If worn with a veil, fine.'

GEOFFREY BEENE

The master of easy American luxury

In the 1970s, Geoffrey Beene (1924–2004) was known and loved in America as much for his genteel Southern manner as for being the designer who had perfected his own ideal for a relaxed easy fit. He rejected the tailored formality of blazers and pleated trousers in favour of elements he would make his own: jumpsuits, pyjama pants, chemise shirt dresses and tunic blouses. And yet, New York's cerebral minimalist was just as well known for his luxurious evening wear, and established a loyal following among ladies on the social circuit who knew just how to make an entrance in his signature polka dot tulle.

Everything he designed had a handcrafted, artisanal quality. This near-couture quality combined with his modern, easy aesthetic made him one of New York's best-known and most respected designers. 'I have never liked rigid clothes,' he said. 'I like freedom. I am an American. I love sweatshirts, skirt and loafers, and I have never deviated from the premise of freedom and effortlessness.'

Geoffrey Beene believed that the future of clothes lay in perfecting synthetics. He was one of ten leading designers approached by DuPont to promote a new synthetic, Qiana. He chose to have the yarn made up into satin velour. 'Working with this material proved to me that synthetics could be perfected, for it was exactly like a pure silk velour, only it did not crease.'

In 1974 the designer launched Beene Bag, a marketing innovation for the time. It was a cheaper line that sold widely and was used to subsidize the creative virtuosity of his main collection. One of Beene's greatest contributions was the respect he earned in Europe for American fashion. In 1976 he took a Beene Bag fashion show to Milan, showing young, sporty separates in inexpensive materials such as mattress ticking. But the end of the show the Italians had enthusiastically come round to the idea that Americans could do more than just jeans.

At a time when women's fashion was heavily influenced by menswear, Geoffrey Beene was experimenting with an easy, relaxed fit. He rejected mannish elements such as blazers and trousers in favour of softer elements that he would make his own: full-skirted dirndls, jumpsuits and flowing pyjamas.

HALSTON

The designer who dressed the sexy 70s

By the late 1970s, Halston was a byword for American style, a combination of minimalism and glamour. His modernizing approach was all-encompassing, from the creation of a modern silhouette to the use of synthetics in high fashion. From perfumes in a signature sinuous bottle to uniforms for flight crews and even the girl scouts, Halston was the colossus of American fashion in the 1970s. Halston clothes were made in luxurious fabrics such as six-ply cashmere and silk charmeuse and were bereft of superfluous trimmings. They were comfortable and easy to wear, ideally suited to the lifestyles of a burgeoning group of jet-set revellers.

Roy Halston Frowick (1932–90) began his career as a milliner to socialites, and famously created the pillbox hat that Jackie Kennedy wore for the 1961 presidential inauguration. His debut fashion show at Bergdorf Goodman was an 18-piece capsule wardrobe of interchangeable pieces. Halston fashion shows were media events. Music played as smiling models sauntered down the runway. His ever-present favourites, including Anjelica Huston, Pat Cleveland and Elsa Peretti, became known as 'the Halstonettes'.

Halston's most famous design was the shirtwaist dress, inspired by a man's long-sleeved shirt. It was made using a synthetic mix of polyester and polyurethane – Ultrasuede. He saw the fabric for the first time in 1971 worn by the Japanese designer Issey Miyake. Halston boasted that his Ultrasuede dresses could be washed in a machine. About 50,000 of those dresses were sold, and Ultrasuede for many years became a fashion staple.

In 1973, Halston was included in a presentation of leading US and French designers in Versailles. Halston was a huge hit, his luxurious simplicity receiving a standing ovation from audience and peers alike, Yves Saint Laurent included. His popularity in the 1970s made him a celebrity, and most famously he was a fixture among the Studio 54 set. Bianca Jagger (opposite) and Liza Minnelli, Elizabeth Taylor and Martha Graham were friends and clients.

In 1978 Halston moved his salon to the 21st floor of the Olympic Tower, New York. With the spires of St Patrick's Cathedral towering behind his desk and a red carpet woven with double Hs, it was a setting fit for a superstar.

For both the fashion insider and the casual observer, Halston evokes visions of languid luxury. He dominated and defined an era: the sexy 70s. He draped them in lamé, wrapped them in cashmere, enveloped them in jersey, decorated them with Elsa Peretti jewellery and upholstered them in Ultrasuede.

VIVIENNE WESTWOOD

Leading the charge of a disenchanted generation

1977

Vivienne Westwood first became a fashion designer in the 1970s. She had been a primary school teacher until she met Malcolm McLaren, who as manager of the Sex Pistols became the most notorious man in London. As McLaren came up with ideas, Vivienne turned them into clothes.

The punk 'style in revolt' was a deliberately 'revolting style' that incorporated into fashion various offensive or threatening things such as tampons, razor blades and lavatory chains. It was a cultural correction – a necessary reset that continues to inspire great music, art and fashion to this day. John Lydon of the Sex Pistols remembered: 'Early 70s Britain was a very depressing place: run-down, trash on the streets, total unemployment – everybody was on strike. The education system told you that if you came from the wrong side of the tracks […] then you had no hope in hell.'

Westwood's confrontational dressing captured the essence of punk. Clothes became a subversive weapon for kids who were never going to drink cocktails on Sunset Boulevard. The guy on the bus in an 'Anarchy in the UK' T-shirt had impact. Punk happened on the street not in the pages of a magazine. Kids refused to be beguiled by glossy images and hand-outs of style and culture.

Westwood and McLaren turned their 50s revival shop Let It Rock into one of the most notorious fetish shops in history. It became Sex in 1975, announcing itself in 4-foot-tall hot-pink foam letters mounted directly on the graffiti-covered storefront. It sold 'rubber for the street, rubber for the office'.

Westwood called her work 'clothes for heroes'. And at the time, you had to be pretty brave to wear them. Punks made a spectacle of themselves on the street, a show of force inciting opposition. But the irony of bondage was mostly lost on the authorities. The designer felt an affinity with Coco Chanel. 'Chanel probably designed for the same reasons I do: irritation with orthodox ways of thinking. She was a street fashion designer.'

Punk put London back on the fashion map for the first time since its swinging days in 1965.

Vivienne Westwood and Malcolm McLaren, pioneers of Brit punk.

Zandra Rhodes (1940–) had an impeccable fashion pedigree. Her mother had been *première d'atelier* (head of the workroom) at the House of Worth in Paris, and after she returned to England taught fashion at one of the country's leading colleges. Zandra's passion was textiles. She branched into fashion only because she had to show the wary market how her fabrics could be used. 'The patterns were considered too extreme, so I had to think how to win people around,' she recalls.

For Rhodes, silhouette was always going to play a supporting role to the virtuosity of the fabric and her head-turning use of colour. In 1970 she created her felt 'Dinosaur coat' with seams pinked and turned inside out, and in 1971 she created her first 'ripped' dress. It was towards the end of the decade, however, that she really came into her own.

This was a tumultuous time in Britain. In 1977, the year of the Queen's Silver Jubilee, royalist London jostled with punk London. The country was in an economic crisis and disaffected youth expressed their rage and frustration in music and fashion. Rhodes presented a 'punk' collection: a glamorization of the punk look with ripped and zipped evening dresses, complete with jewelled safety pins. With the collection, she became an instant fashion star both in America and the UK.

Overnight, Rhodes became the doyenne of British haute punk. The controversial creativity of punk provided rich pickings and quickly became a catwalk commodity that inspired the French avant-garde designers in Paris, too. Vivienne Westwood berated the Europeans for ripping off her ideas, but commented, 'I didn't mind Zandra copying punk rock because she did it in her own way.'

Rhodes once remarked that she didn't see why holes in cloths should be so inherently frightening. Didn't lace have holes, too?

Rhodes' work has always appealed to 'alternative thinkers', and like Elsa Schiaparelli she consolidated the link between fashion and art. But this was far from street fashion. In Rhodes' version of punk, the ripped garments were carefully pinned together with 18-carat-gold safety pins from Cartier.

STUDIO 54

The biggest party ever thrown

Founded by Steve Rubell and Ian Schrager in 1977, Studio 54 was an enormous discotheque which, during its heyday, was packed with thousands of people. The crowd included the rich and famous as well as the unknown but interesting, and embodied the glamorous decadence of the time. Drugs and sex of seemingly endless quantities and varieties were easily available.

A team of architects, theatrical lighting impresarios, set designers and florists was employed to convert what had been an abandoned theatre into an ever-changing playground. Special 'one night only' performances by the hottest musical acts were regularly scheduled. Studio 54 took the nightclub scene by storm, and was an instant, headline-grabbing success.

There was no VIP room. Everyone shared the same dance floor and banquette – if you could get in, that is. The club was famous for its notorious door policy. Rubell carefully selected the perfect mix of people to enter. On any night you might find Yves Saint Laurent catching up with Halston; Michael Jackson hanging out with Liza Minnelli and Liz Taylor; Mick and Bianca Jagger (see opposite), Jerry Hall, Diana Vreeland, Farrah Fawcett-Major, Truman Capote, Elton John, John Travolta, Margaux Hemingway, Mikhail Baryshnikov, Grace Jones, Salvador Dalí, Brooke Shields, Donald Trump, Francesco Scavullo, Joan Collins, Cher, Martha Graham and Debbie Harry.

Andy Warhol said that Studio 54 was 'a dictatorship at the door and a democracy inside'. Once in, you were a star. Rubell and Schrager gave event planner Robert Isabell his first break with the planning of a memorable New Year's Eve party. Isabell had four tons of glitter dumped in a 4-inch layer on the dance floor. Schrager described it as like 'standing on stardust'.

Even when the club was shut down by the police for want of a liquor licence, it stayed open selling fruit juice, and queues still wound around the block.

In 1977, '54' grossed an estimated $7 million. It was as famous for sex and drugs as for the phenomenal light-and-sound show. In 1978, after Rubell publicly bragged about the club's profits, armed federal agents raided the premises. The party was well and truly over.

KATE BUSH

Music's first high priestess of the New Age

1978

Kate Bush (1958–), queen of the concept album, is a cult pop star in the truest sense of the term. Her first single, 'Wuthering Heights', inspired by the Emily Brontë novel, was the song that launched her career in 1978. Since then her songs have gradually evolved into lengthy set pieces full of drama and atmosphere.

Her arrival on the music scene coincided with the arrival of punk, and with her wild hair and New Age ideas she seemed every bit as anarchic. No one before her had engaged fans quite so earnestly in debates about astrology, reincarnation, UFOs and synchronicity.

While punk expressed head banging rage, Bush struggled to make the connection between her music, imagery and ideas. She came from a classical background with training in dance and mime. She described her costumes and makeup as masks to hide behind, 'I don't want to be up there on the stage being me,' she told *Musician* magazine. 'I don't think I'm that interesting. What I want to do is to be the person that's in the song.'

Kate Bush is probably most famous for the white-robed ghost of Cathy in the promotional video made for her 1978 hit single, Wuthering Heights, which mesmerized the British public for the four gloomy January weeks that it held its No 1 spot. Performing in a Victorian nightgown, the 'White Dress' Cathy video was mostly responsible for promoting the image of 'Bush the ethereal hippy'. But even in her spandex and batwing years, she has often appeared as much medium as message, channeling spirits that seem slightly beyond her control.

In 1979, Kate Bush undertook the first and only tour of her career so far. Her innovative musical style was matched by an on-stage persona that was by turns dreamily romantic and sexually provocative.

98

MARGAUX HEMINGWAY

The face of a generation

Six feet tall in her bare feet – five foot twelve, she would often quip – Margaux Hemingway (1954–96), granddaughter of the writer Ernest Hemingway, rolled into New York, a 19-year-old graduate from Idaho on an internship with a local PR company. While she was having tea at her hotel, she was spotted by Errol Wetson, a hamburger-chain heir – 'He knocked on the door of my suite with a rose and a bottle of champagne,' she said, 'and I fell in love.'

Wetson became her Svengali, advising her what to wear and taking her to the right parties. With her sporty outdoor looks and those caterpillar eyebrows, she became an instant success, and overnight tweezers became a thing of the past. Within a year, Hemingway was on the covers of *Vogue* and *Time* magazine. On 16 June 1975, the cover of *Time* dubbed her one of the 'new beauties', while the September issue of American *Vogue* christened Hemingway as 'New York's New Supermodel'. In the same year, Joe Eula, the fashion illustrator at the epicentre of the Halston set, called her 'the face of a generation'.

Her meteoric rise to fame peaked when she became the spokesmodel for Fabergé's Babe perfume and landed the first ever million-dollar deal. She became a Studio 54 regular, carousing alongside celebrities such as Liza Minnelli, Halston, Bianca Jagger, Andy Warhol and Grace Jones.

Hemingway's looks were so distinctive that when she went to a club she could be sure of instant access to VIP circles. 'I don't need any I.D.,' she joked, 'I have my eyebrows.' Her incandescence started to fade when she made her film debut in the 1976 drama *Lipstick* alongside her then 14-year-old sister, Mariel. Margaux's performance was panned. Mariel, though, got a Golden Globe nomination for 'Best Newcomer' that year and went on to star in Woody Allen's *Manhattan*.

Hemingway, granddaughter of Ernest Hemingway, changed the spelling of her name from the usual Margot to Margaux, in honour of the wine alleged to have inspired her conception.

STEVIE NICKS

Rock's eccentrically dressed bohemian goddess

1978

It's impossible to talk about 1970s fashion without bringing up that eccentrically dressed bohemian goddess, Stevie Nicks (1948–). With her shaggy blonde hair, top hats, draped jackets and slouchy boots, Stevie is the quintessential 1970s style icon to whom anyone in need of a little hippie inspiration turns.

The look came about as a disguise. 'My stage fright was and is terrible,' she says. 'So adding pressure with clothes was ridiculous. I didn't want to think about it. So I designed my little uniform. I knew from the beginning that I wanted to be famous when I was 70 and realized that being terribly sexy couldn't last.'

Her brief to Margi Kent, who still designs much of her wardrobe, was to create 'something urchin-like out of *Great Expectations* or *A Tale of Two Cities*', a chiffon-like, raggedy skirt that would still look beautiful with black velvet platform boots. 'We came up with the outfit: a Jantzen leotard, a little chiffon wrap blouse, a couple of little short jackets, two skirts and boots.' And, of course, the shawl, which is an essential part of her concert uniform. 'A shawl is a great prop,' says the star, who is just five foot one. 'It makes for big gestures. If you want to be seen at the back of that arena, you have to have very big movements.'

In their 2001 Fall collections, Anna Sui, Betsey Johnson and Oscar de la Renta seemed to invoke Nicks' look with bohemian skirts and ruffled shirts. And in 2010, once again, she was a key catwalk inspiration.

The fairy godmother of the gypsy romantic look, Stevie Nicks has inspired generations of fans to drape themselves in chiffon and velvet and add feathers to their accessory kit. She has become a reluctant fashion icon, responsible for keeping up sales of vintage white lace over three decades.

DISCO

A decade's energy let loose on the dance floor

Disco was born in 1970 with the opening of a club called The Loft in New York City, and pretty much died in 1980 with the proliferation of suburban clubs where dancing baby-boomers copied moves and looks from the 1977 film *Saturday Night Fever*. For the first eight years, however, disco was an underground movement that emerged from African American and gay clubs in New York City. Legendary clubs such as Studio 54 became the definition of 1970s glamour, with a nightly VIP crowd that included Michael Jackson, Andy Warhol, Bianca Jagger, Liza Minnelli and the designer Halston.

Being at a disco was like being on stage. The greatest dancers wore what got them noticed. A shiny satin shirt or second-skin bodysuit and sequin jackets were staples of the disco wardrobe – your clothes could not be outshone by the glitter on those dance-floor mirror balls. Lycra leggings in hot colours and skin-tight stretch jeans were staples of the unisex wardrobe, and were often adapted from the kit of professional modern dancers. Gold-lamé, leopard-skin and white fabrics that glowed under the ultraviolet light were perfect for posing.

The liberation movement made it a woman's prerogative to wear whatever she felt like on any particular day. In disco the sexual liberation pioneered in the 1960s was embraced, but dressed up as a glamorous urban version in halter-neck tops, sequin bandeau tops and stretch satin cat suits.

The storyline of *Saturday Night Fever* sums up disco's seductive power for the man (or woman) in the street – Tony, the working-class Italian-American who was a hardware salesman by day and a disco king by night, was not the only one who seized the glamorous way out of the tedious daily grind. Thanks to disco, clubs got dress codes and door screening policies. Suddenly you had to look the part to gain entry to that one night of paradise.

Disco had its detractors, of course. Punk scorned it, equating it with the cabaret culture of Weimar Germany for its ignorance of social ills and its escapism.

With her big hair, false eye lashes, plunging neck-lines, gold lamé and second-skin sequined dresses, Donna Summer was the undisputed 'Queen of Disco'. Her gospel-trained voice was a driving force of the sound with hits like 'Love to Love You Baby', 'I Feel Love' and 'Last Dance'.

PAT CLEVELAND

Catwalk queen of the disco era

1979

Before the term supermodel ever graced a headline, Pat Cleveland (1963–) was a pioneering beauty, and she is now considered one of fashion's first black 'supermodels'. She was the catwalk queen of the disco era. The black-Cherokee-Irish stunner took Paris and the world by storm with a runway walk that was like no other. Whether working for Halston or Yves Saint Laurent, she owned the catwalk, twirling and dancing and leaving her audience speechless.

Pat was discovered in 1967 by Carrie Donovan, who was then a fashion editor at US *Vogue*. The 14-year-old student at Manhattan's LaGuardia High School of Performing Arts had a rocky start, but went on to become every designer's runway dream. Back then, black models were not considered as assets in the mainstream fashion industry, while successful models specialized in either print work for magazines or the runway – rarely both. Pat was a mainstream black model who excelled on the catwalk *and* the magazine covers.

Cleveland moved to Paris in 1971, and got a career-defining break in the winter of 1973. To celebrate the restoration of Louis XIV's opulent chateau of Versailles, a small coterie of American designers (Bill Blass, Stephen Burrows, Anne Klein, Halston and Oscar de la Renta) took part in a fashion gala opposite France's undisputed kings of fashion (Hubert de Givenchy, Yves Saint Laurent, Emanuel Ungaro and Pierre Cardin). The Americans' minimalist staging and cast of black models, including Billie Blair, Norma Jean Darden, Bethann Hardison and of course Pat Cleveland, made the baroque French presentation look instantly dated. The event became known as the 'Battle of Versailles' and the Americans emerged triumphant. Cleveland became a star.

One of the original 'Halstonettes', Cleveland held court through the 70s at Studio 54 where she served as muse for Andy Warhol. But she was also the consummate professional, becoming an inspiration for Thierry Mugler, Paco Rabanne, Yves Saint Laurent, Karl Lagerfeld and Franco Moschino.

106

INDEX

PICTURE CREDITS

FURTHER READING

Anscombe, Isabelle (1978),
Not Another Punk! Book,
Urizen Books

Bluttal, Steven and Mears,
Patricia (2011), *Halston*,
Phaidon Press Ltd

Bowie, Angela and
Carr, Patrick (2000),
*Backstage Passes: Life on the
Wild Side with David Bowie*,
Cooper Square Publishers
Inc.,U.S.

Devlin, Polly (1979),
*Vogue Book of Fashion
Photography*,
Simon & Schuster

Howell, Georgina (1978),
*In Vogue: Sixty Decades of
Fashion*, Penguin Books Ltd

Jones, Dylan (1990), *Haircults*,
Thames & Hudson Ltd

Turner, Alwyn W. (2007),
Biba: The Biba Experience,
Antique Collectors' Club Ltd

Von Furstenberg, Diane
(1979), *How to Become a
More Attractive, Confident
and Sensual Woman*,
Simon & Schuster

CREDITS

First published in 2012
by Conran Octopus Ltd
a part of Octopus Publishing
Group, Endeavour House,
189 Shaftesbury Avenue,
London WC2H 8JY
www.octopusbooks.co.uk

An Hachette UK Company
www.hachette.co.uk

Distributed in the US by
Hachette Book Group USA,
237 Park Avenue, New York,
NY 10017 USA

Distributed in Canada by
Canadian Manda Group,
165 Dufferin Street, Toronto,
Ontario, Canada M6K 3H6

British Library Cataloguing-
in-Publication Data.
A catalogue record for this
book is available from the
British Library.

Text written by: Paula Reed

Publisher: Alison Starling
Consultant Editor:
Deyan Sudjic
Senior Editor: Sybella Stephens
Editor: Robert Anderson
Art Director: Jonathan Christie
Design: Untitled
Picture Research:
Anne-Marie Hoines
& Sara Rumens
Production: Caroline Alberti

ISBN: 978 1 84091 605 8
Printed in China